What Do Clouds Tell Us?

by **LAURA HULBERT**

With the Editors of TIME For Kids

Table of Contents

Chapter One

How Clouds Form

What forms, or makes, clouds? The Sun heats the water on Earth. Some water becomes a gas called **water vapor**. Water vapor goes up into the sky. It gets cooler. It turns back into tiny drops of water. Clouds have many tiny drops of water.

Some clouds are fat and puffy. Some clouds are thin and flat. Some clouds are white. Some clouds are gray. Some clouds are almost black. Clouds can show us what the weather will be like later.

In this book you will learn how to "read" clouds.

Chapter Two

How to Read Clouds

These are **cirrus** (SIR-uhs) clouds. *Cirrus* means "curly." Some people think these clouds look like horse tails. What do you think?

Cirrus clouds

We see these thin clouds high in the sky.
We see them on a sunny day. They tell us
the wind is changing. They tell us maybe it
will rain tomorrow.

These are **stratus** (STRAYT-uhs) clouds. *Stratus* means "stretched," or "spread." Stratus clouds hide the Sun. They make the sky dark and gray.

Stratus clouds

It is a warm sunny day. Do you see stratus clouds? We will have rain soon. It is a cold winter day. Do you see stratus clouds? We will have snow soon. Stratus clouds close to the ground make **fog**.

Fog

These are **cumulus** (KYEW-myuh-luhs) clouds. *Cumulus* means "heap" or "pile." We can draw cumulus clouds.

Sometimes these puffy white clouds are low. When we see cumulus clouds and a blue sky, we have a nice, sunny day.

Cumulus clouds

**Tall cumulus clouds
bring rain.**

Sometimes cumulus clouds grow tall. They go high in the sky. Get your umbrella! It will rain soon. Maybe we will have a thunderstorm.

Nimbus (NIM-buhs) clouds are dark gray. *Nimbus* means "rain cloud." Some nimbus clouds are flat stratus clouds.

Nimbus clouds

Some nimbus clouds are puffy cumulus clouds. They bring thunder and lightning. They bring big rainstorms.

Puffy nimbus clouds bring rain.

Chapter 3

What Clouds Say

Long ago, sailors watched the clouds a lot. Can they go out to sea today? Farmers looked at clouds, too. Can they cut the hay today? They did not have TV. They did not have a weather report.

What do these
clouds mean?

People made sayings about what the
clouds told them. Read this saying. What
kind of cloud is it?

*"When clouds look like black smoke,
A wise man will put on his cloak."*

That is right! Dark nimbus clouds tell you
that you will need your raincoat today.

What kind of weather will we have tomorrow? Look up in the sky. What do the clouds tell you?

Glossary

 cirrus (SIR-uhs) thin, curly clouds way up in the sky *(page 4)*

 cumulus (KYEW-myuh-luhs) puffy white clouds *(page 8)*

 fog (FOG) a cloud close to the ground *(page 7)*

 nimbus (NIM-buhs) a dark cloud; it tells us rain is coming *(page 10)*

 stratus (STRAYT-uhs) thin, flat clouds; they hide the Sun *(page 6)*

 water vapor (WAW-tuhr VAY-puhr) water that becomes a gas *(page 2)*

Index